# 中 国 登 长 城 纪 念

## A COMMEMORATIVE CERTIFICATE FOR ASCENDING THE GREAT WALL IN CHINA

不 到 長 城 非 好 漢

NOT A PLUCKY HERO UNTIL ONE REACHES THE GREAT WALL

我 登 上 了 長 城

I HAVE ASCENDED THE GREAT WALL

颁 发 给
This is to certify that ....................................................................

攀 登 长 城 日 期
did climb the Great Wall on ....................................................

颁发者
Issued by

# 前　言

在中華大地上，舉世聞名的萬里長城，象一條奔騰的巨龍，騰起于鴨綠江畔，向西越過巍巍的群山，茫茫的草原，跨過浩瀚的大漠，奔向白雪皚皚的天山之麓。以它異常艱巨的工程和磅礴的氣勢把北國風光點綴得更加絢麗多彩。長城是中國古代的偉大建築，被列爲世界建築奇迹之一，載入世界文明史冊。一九八八年被聯合國定爲世界文化遺產。萬里長城是中華各族人民血汗和智慧的結晶，也可以說是中國歷史上的一座豐碑，成爲中華民族的象征。

長城在中國歷史上奔騰飛躍了二千多年，至今依然氣勢磅礴，雄偉壯觀。美國阿波羅11號宇宙飛船登上月球時，宇航員興奮的說："在月球上用肉眼只能最清晰的辨認中國的萬里長城。"萬里長城的工程量確實惊人！據粗略的估計，若將明朝修築長城所用的磚石、土方，築成一道寬一米，高五米的大牆，能繞地球一周有余。如果用來鋪建寬五米，厚三十五厘米的公路，可以繞地球三、四周。中國的萬里長城眞不愧是世界的奇迹！

長城是中國古代偉大的軍事防禦工程，公元前221年秦始皇統一中國後，把以前各國之間的長城拆除，將原先秦、趙、燕三國北面的長城連接起來以抵禦北方的游牧民族。這一長城西起臨洮（今甘肅岷縣），東至遼東，全長一萬余華里，爲一道堅不可摧的北方防禦體系，從此萬里長城就聞名于世了。到了漢代長城比秦代又有所發展，東起鴨綠江畔，往西一直延伸到今天新疆的羅布泊，全長超過二萬華里，這是長城歷史上最長的時期。長城歷經變遷，到了明代又一次大規模的修建長城。東起鴨綠江口西至甘肅嘉峪關總長度爲一萬二千七百多華里，今天我們所見到的長城大都是明代所修建的。長城大都建于山嶺之顚，沿着山脊把蜿蜒無盡的山勢勾畫出優美的曲綫輪廓，城上無數堅實雄壯的敵臺，與矗立于嶺上的烽火臺遙相呼應，萬里長城以它磅礴的氣勢奔騰在崇山峻嶺之中，成百座雄關、險口，成千上萬的雄壯敵臺、峰火臺連成一體。令人們嘆爲觀止，感嘆中華民族的勤勞、智慧、和傑出偉大。

長城從它開始修築時起，逐步完善改進，直到它完成了歷史上的作用。長城是伴隨着中國整個漫長歷史而興衰的，到了現代長城已失去了它原有的防禦作用，自然的風雨侵蝕和人爲的破壞，使長城處于逐漸殘毀之中。建國以來，長城被列爲重點維修項目，現已修復了長城多處重要地段，長城又重展昔日雄姿。而今，中國長城已成爲世界旅游勝地。長城不僅是中國的驕傲，也是全人類文化的瑰寶，更是聯系世界各國人民的友好紐帶。我社在鄧小平同志"愛我中華，修我長城"題詞10周年之際出版的這本畫冊，以著名攝影家成大林所拍攝的大量寶貴的圖片把長城的風貌展現在讀者面前。望能給世界各國的朋友們以美的享受！

1994.5

# Preface

The world-famous Great Wall lies in China as an enormous flying dragon. It starts from Yalu River bank in the east, through high mountains, vast steppes and boundless deserts, to reach at the snow-covered Tianshan Mountains in the west. The extraordinary difficult engineering and imposing manner of the Great Wall give a more magnificent scenery to Northern China. Great architecture of ancient China, the Great Wall is considered one of the wonders of the world, it holds a very important place in the history of the world civilisation. In 1988, the UN designated it one of the world's greatest cultural heritages. A crystallization of blood, sweat and intelligence, the Great Wall is not only a historical monument of China, but also a symbol of the Chinese People.

The Great Wall, with a history of more than 2000 years, still keeps its imposing manner and looks magnificent today. When they arrived on the moon, American astronauts of the space-shuttle Apollo II said exitedly that the only man-made structure to be visible from the moon was the Great Wall of China. The engineering of the Great Wall is astonishing! According to a rough estimation, if you took all the bricks and rocks used in the Great Wall of the Ming Dynasty and built a wall 1 meter wide and 5 meters high, it wouid go around the earth once or more. If a highway 5 meters wide and 35 centimeters thick was built with those materials, it could go around the earth 3 or 4 times. The Great Wall is really a miracle of the worid!

The Great Wall is a great military defence project of ancien China. When Qin Shi Huang unified China in 221 B.C., he linked up the northern walls of the Qin, Zhao and Yan Kindoms to protect from the invasions of nomadic tribes of the North, while demolishing others. Stretching from Lintao (now Mingxian in Gansu Province) in the west to Liaodong in the east, the Great wall had at that time a lenghth of more than 5,000 kilometers. As a solid defense system, it became more and more famous. The Great Wall was extended and rebuilt in the Han Dynasty. Streching from Yalu River bank in the east to Luobupo Lake in what is now Xinjiang autonomous region, it has a total lenghth of more than 10, 000 kilometers, the longest in its history. Having gone through many changes, the Great Wall was reconstructed in a large scale in the Ming Dynasty. Extending westward from the Yalu River bank to Jiayuguan in Gansu Province, the Great Wall as we know today is mostly the construction of the Ming Dynasty with a total lenghth of about 6,350 kilometers. The Great Wall was built at top of the mountains, depicting beautiful curves of their ridges. Meandering along high mountains and deep valleys with its hundreds of passes and thousands of forts, watch towers in a hamony, the Great Wall is really magnificent, one can not help admiring the deligence, intelligence and greatness of the Chinese People.

The Great Wall had never ceased to be perfected from its beginning to its end of the role as a means of defence. Rising and declining along with the long history of China, the Great Wall lost gradually its original function, the erosion of wind and rain with the man-made dammage dilapidated the Great Wall. After the foundation of the People's Republic of China, the Great Wall was assigned one of the most important historical sites to be repaired. After restoration of many of its important sections, the Great Wall has resumed its imposing manner, it is now an important tourist attraction for people all over the world. The Great Wall is not only a pride of China, but also a tresor of the world civilisation and a link between peoples all over the world. In commemoration of the writing "love China and repair the Great Wall" by Mr. Deng Xiaoping, we published this photo album, in which famous photographer Mr. Cheng Dalin unfolds before us a variety of aspects of the Great Wall through his precious photos. We hope friends all over the world will enjoy it!

May 1994

# 前　書

　中国の大地において、世を挙げて、その名の聞こえる万里の長城が空を闊歩する巨竜のように、鴨緑江のほとりから西に向けて飛立ち、聳え立つ山山やはてもしない大草原を越え、広大な大漠を跨り、真っ白な雪に覆われる天山の麓に飛んで行った。その困難極まる麗大な工事と天を衝く勢いは北国の景色をいっそう絢爛たるものにしたのである。長城は中国古代の偉大な建築であり、世界建築史上の奇跡の一つとして世界文明の歴史に載せられ、一九八八年国連によって世界文化遺産と指定された。万里の長城は中国各民族人民の血と汗と智慧の結晶であり、中国の歴史における朽ない紀念碑とも言え、中華民族のシンボルとなっている。

　長城は中国の歴史において、二千年以上も活躍し、今日になってもあいかわらず勢いよく、雄大壮観そのものである。アメリカの宇宙船アポロが月に登った時、宇航士は「月で人間の目ではっきり見えたのは中国の万里の万城だけだった」と感激した。万里の長城の工事量はほんとうに驚くべきものであった。大雑把な統計によると、明の時代に長城を修築するのに使った石、煉瓦、土で、広さ１メートル、高さ５メートルの垣をつくるなら、地球を一周して余りがあるほどつくれるそうである。また広さ５メートル、厚さ35ミリの道をつくるなら、地球を三周も四周もできるほどである。中国の万里の長城はまことに世界の奇跡たるに恥じないものである。

　長城は中国古代の偉大な軍事防御工事でもあった。紀元前221年、秦の始皇帝は中国を統一してからそれまでに存在していた各国間の長城をすべて取り除けて、元の秦、趙、燕などの三国の北側にあった長城を結ばせ、北方の遊牧民族を防御した。この長城は西は臨洮（今の甘粛省岷県にあたる）から始まり、東は遼東まで全長１万華里余りもあって、堅固でうちやぶることのできない北方防御体系となり、万里の長城もその時から世に名が聞こえるようになっ

た。漢の時代になって、秦の時代よりさらに発展させ、東は鴨緑江のほとりから、西はずっといまの新疆羅布泊まで延ばされ、全長は２万華里も越え、長城の史上最長期をなした。その後も長城は変遷をくりかえ、明の時代にふたたび大規模な長城修築が行われた。東は鴨緑江の入江から、西は甘粛省の嘉峪関まで、全長１万2700華里余りもあり、今日われわれが見える長城のほとんどはこの時につくられたものである。長城は大抵山の頂上につくられ、山の脊に沿って、曲りくねって尽きることのない山山の美しい曲線を浮彫りにした。長城の上にある無数の堅固で雄大な櫓と山頂に聳え立つ烽火台が遥かに向いあって呼応しあった。万里の長城はその雄大な勢いで、険しい山山の間を疾走し、数百の関所、要害や何千何万という堅固な櫓や烽火台と一体となって、中華民族の勤勉、智慧と偉大さで人人を感服させた。

　長城はつくられた時からくりかえされる改築と修繕を経て、歴史的な役割を完遂させるまで、ずっと中国の長い歴史と一緒にあゆみ、盛衰をともにしてきた。近代になって、長城はすでに本来の防御の役割をなくし、自然の風化と人為的な破壊で崩壊寸前となっていた。新中国が成立し、長城は重点的な修繕プロジェクトとして見なされた。すでに大事な部分が多く修復され、長城はふたたび昔の雄姿を見せるようになった。いま中国の長城はすでに世界的な観光地となった。長城は中国の誇りだけでなく、全人類の文化的珍宝でもあり、また世界各国人民をむすびつく友好的なきずなでもあった。わが社は鄧小平同志の「わが中華を愛し、わが長城を修復しよう」という題字の10周年にあたって、この写真集を出版し、著名なカメラマン成大林氏が取られた大量な貴重な写真でもって、長城の風采を読者の皆様の前に再現したいと思う。世界各国の友人の皆様に気入れていただければ幸いである。

一九九四.五

# Préface

La Grande Muraille, célèbre dans le monde entier, se dresse comme un énorme dragon en Chine. Elle part près du Fleuve Yalu, traversant vers l'ouest des hautes montagnes, des vastes steppes et des deserts sans bornes, pour aboutir au pied des Montagnes Tianshan couvertes de la neige. Les travaux extrêmement pénibles de la Grande Muraille et sa belle prestance embellient le Nord de la Chine. Gigantesque construction de la Chine antique, la Grande Muraille est considerée comme un miracle dans l'histoire de construction du monde, elle occupe une place très importante dans la civilisation du monde. En 1988, l'Organisation des Nations unies l'a désignée comme un des grands héritages culturels du monde. Resultat de la sagesse, du sang et de la sueur du peuple Chinois, la Grande Muraille est non seulement un monument historique Chinois, mais aussi un symbole du peuple Chinois.

Bien que la Grande Muraille ait plus de deux milles ans d'histoire, elle garde encore sa belle prestance. Après avoir atterri sur la Lune, les astronautes américains de la navette astronomique Apollo II dirent que la seule chose ils avaient pu distinquer par l'oeil sur la Lune était la Grande Muraille de la Chine. Les travaux de construction de la Grande Muraille sont vraiment ètonnants! D'après l'estimation simple, si l'on construise un mur d'une largeur d'un mètre et une hauteur de cinq mètres avec des grosse briques et des blocs de pierres utilisés par la Grande Muraille de la Dynastie des Ming, il pourrait faire un tour de la Terre. Si l'on construise avec ces matériaux une autoroute d'une largeur de cinq mètres et une épaisseur de trente-cinq centimètres, elle pourrait faire deux ou trois tours de la Terre. La Grande Muraille est vraiment une miracle du monde!

La Grande Muraille est une grande ouvrage de défense militaire de la Chine antique. Après avoir unifié la Chine en 221 av. J.-C., l'empreur Shihuandi de la Dynastie des Qin, relia les diverses murailles des anciens Royaumes de Qin, Zhao et Yan le long de leur frontière nord des murailles pour se protéger des incursions des tribus nomades, tout en détruisant les autres murailles des anciens royaumes. S'étandant, de l'ouest à l'est, de Lintao (aujourd'hui Minxian dans le Gansu) à Liaodong, la Grande Muraille eut une longueur de plus de 5,000 kilomètres à cette époque. Rampart imprenable au Nord de la Chine, elle devenait de plus en plus connue du monde. Consolidée et prolongée sous la Dynastie des Han, la Grande Muraille fut mesurée plus de dix milles kilomètres, partant auprès du Fleuve Yalu à l'est pour aboutir jusqu'au Lac Luobupo de Xinjiang à l'ouest, c'était la plus longue muraille ever connue dans son histoire. La Grande Muraille fut reconstruite d'une grande envergure sous la Dynastie des Ming après avoir connu becoup de changements. S'étendant, de l'est à l'ouest, de la gorge du Fleuve Yalu à la Passe Jiayuguan, la Grande Muraille que nous voyons aujourd'hui est à peu près la Grande Muraille de la Dynsatie des Ming avec une longueur de 6,350 kilomètres. La plupart de la Grande Muraille est construite sur les crêtes de montagnes, decrivant ainsi leurs belles lignes courbes. Serpentant dans les hautes montagnes et les vallers profondes, la Grande Muraille est plus étonnante avec ses centaines de passes et ses milliers de fortins et avant-postes. On ne peut s'empêcher devant elle d'admirer la diligence, la sagesse et la grandeur du peuple Chinois.

La Grande Muraille n'a pas cessé de se perfectionner depuis sa construction jusqu'à la fin de son role comme un moyen de défence. Connaissant des périodes de grandeur et decadence le long de la longue histoire de Chine, la Grande Muraillle a perdu graduellement sa foncton originale, elle a été dans une condition pitoyable à cause de l'erosion de vent et de pluie et la destruction causée by des gens. Après la fondation de la Republique Populaire de Chine, la Grande Muraille a été désignée comme un des plus importants sites historiques de la Chine à être protégés. Maintenant beaucoup de ses tronçons importants ont été reconstruits, la Grande Muraille s'est remise à sa prestance d'auparavant. Elle devient aujourd'hui un des importants sites touristiques du monde. Comme un lien entre les peuples du monde, elle est non seulement l'orgueil de la Chine, mais aussi le trésor du monde entier. A l'occassion que M. Deng Xiaopin a écrit il y a dix ans le slogan "aimons la Chine et reconstruisons la Grande Muraille", notre société a publié cet album de photos prises pat le célèbre photograqhe M. Cheng Dalin. Nous espérons que ces photos precieuses offfrent aux lecteurs des differents aspects de la Grande Muraille et que les amis du monde entier puissent en avoir la jouissance!

Mai 1994

▲ 長城秋艷
The Great Wall in autumn
長城の秋景色
La Grande Muraille en automne

龍臥翠嶺
The Great Wall on luxuriant mountains
緑の山嶺に伏せる龍
La Grande Muraille sur des montagnes exubérantes

▶ 長城綠茵
The Great Wall nestled in
green
長城をみどりの背景に置く
La Grande Muraille tapie dans une
couleur verte

緑毯臥龍
Dragons on green blankets
緑に囲まれた長城
Dragons sur des couvertures vertes

▶ 臥龍戲水
Drangon plays in water
ドラゴンが水をあそぶ
Le dragon s'amuse dans l'eau

峰高城更高 ▼
Wall atop high mountains
高い峰の上にそらに高い城がある
La Grande Muraille au dessus de
hautes montagnes

金山嶺夏
Jinshanling in summer
金山嶺の夏
Jinshanling en été

古往今來
Through the age
昔から今末で
De l'antiquité jusqu'à nos
jours

夕照金山嶺
inshanling at sunset
夕日に照る金山嶺
inshanling au coucher du soleil

國色天香
Elegance and fragrance
この国のこの上もない美しさ
La beauté de la nation et le parfum
du soleil

**漢塞日出** ▼
Sunrise beyond wall
長城の内側から見る日の
出
Lever du soleil au–delà de la
Grande Muraille

**城下紅葉**
Red leaves at Foot of Great
Wall
城の下の紅叶
Feuille rouges au pied de la
Grande Muraille

長城素裹
Great Wall wrapped in white
まつ白になつた長城
La Grande Muraille dans la neige

**春城晨霧**
Wall in spring fog
春城の朝霧
La Grande Muraille dans le brouillard au prin-
temps

巨龍騰飛
The Great Wall runs along mountain ridges
飛舞う巨龍
La Grande Muraille serpentant sur des crêtes
de Montagnes

盤山越嶺
The Great Walll winds throngh deep mountains
えんえんと延びる長城
La Grande Muraille s'enroule à travers de hautes montagnes

**敵樓高聳**
A watch tower on the Great Wall
そびえ立つ城塞
Fortins en haut de la Grande Muraille

春山如笑
The Great Wall in May
春の長城
La Grande Muraille au printemps

山陡城高
High wall against steep mountains
険しい山に高い城
La Haute Muraille contre des montagnes escarpées

敵樓林立
Watch towers on the Great Wall
城塞林立
Fortins en haut de la Grande Muraille

嘉峪關拱門
Arched gate of Jiayuguan Pass
嘉峪関のアーチ門
La Porte voutée du Passe Jiayugan

**森嚴壁壘** ▼
A great defense work
鋼鉄のような防壁
Un rempart imprenable

**嘉峪晨光**
Jiayuguan Pass at dawn
嘉峪関に朝日の光
Jiayuguan au point du
jour

春城桃花
Wall dotted with peach blossoms
春の長城に桃の花が咲く
La Grande Muraille parsemée par la
fleur de pêcher

**長城降雪**
Snow falls on the Great Wall
雪が長城に降る
La neige tombe dans la Grande Muraille

潘家口長城
The Great Wall at Panjiakou
潘家口長城
La Grande Muraille à Panjiakou

長城入海
Great Wall dips into sea
長城が海に臨む
La Grande Muraille baigne dans l'eau

古城之夏
Ancient wall in Summer
古城の夏
La muraille ancienne en été

曲城趣藝
Art of zigzag
曲城の趣
L`art des zigzag

► 長城關隘
The Great Wall Pass
長城の関所
Passe de la Grande Muraille

慕田峪秋色
Mutianyu in Autumn
慕田峪の秋景色
Mutianyu en automne

嘉峪關
Jiayuguan

嘉峪關
Jiayuguan

八達嶺之夏
Badaling in Summer
八達嶺の夏
Badaling en été

古城磁
Ancient wall and jagged ro
古城の蘭
La muraille ancienne et des roc
tourme

黄花城之夏
mmer at Huanghua Wall
黄花城の夏
Huanghuachen en été

金山嶺長城雄姿
The Great Wall at Jinshanling
金山嶺長城の雄姿
La Grande Muraille à Jinshanling

長城秋歌
Great Wall in Autumn
秋の長城讚歌
La Grande Muraille en automne

秋映長城
Great Wall in Autu-
mn
長城の秋光
La Grande Muraille en
automne

森嚴壁壘
A great defense work
鋼鉄のような防壁
une ouvrage de défense sur la Grande Muraille

春城晨霧
Wall in spring fog
春城の朝霧
La Grande Muraille dans le brouillard du printemps

長城夕照
Old wall in dusk
夕日が照り返す長城
La Grande Muraille à la nuit tombante

古往今來
Through the ages
昔から今末で
De l'antiguité jusgu'à nos jours

嘉峪關夕輝
Jianyuguan under sun's glow
嘉峪関の夕焼け
Jianyuguan sous des rayons du soleil couchant

金蛇狂舞
A dancing golden snake
舞い狂う金色の蛇
Un serpent d´or en dansant

▲ 敦煌漢長城遺址
Ruins of the Great Wall of the Han Dynasty in Dunhuang
漢の敦煌長城跡
Vestiges de la Grande Muraille de la Dynastie des Han à Dunhuang

八達嶺初雪
An early snowfall at Badaling
八達嶺の初雪
La première neige sur la Grande Muraille

雪覆蒼龍
The Great Wall after snow
雪におおわれた蒼龍
La Grande Muraille après la neige

山舞銀蛇
Silver wall snakes along mountain
山の頂上に踊る銀色の蛇
Un serpent d'argent le long de la montagne

內蒙古長城遺跡
Ruins of the
Great Wall in In-
ner Mogolia
內蒙古長城遺跡
Vestiges de la
Grande Muraille
en Mongolie in-
térieure

天下第一關
NO.1 Pass under heaven
天下一の関所
La première passe du monde

東西馳騁
The Great Wall runs
along moutain ri-
dges from east to
west
東西に走る長城
La Grande Muraille
de l'est à l'ouest

漫山紅遍
The moutains are covered with red leaves in autumn
紅に染めるもみじ
Montagnes couvertes des feuilles rouge en automne

▼ 城下花盛
Bolossoms below wall
長城のふもとに花がいぱい咲く
Les fleurs au pied de la Grande Muraille

長城關隘・紫荊關
The Great Wall Pass－Zijing Pass
長城の関所・紫荊関
La Passe de la Grande Muraille － Zijingguan

長城關隘 • 娘子關
The Great Wall Pass – Niangzi Pass
長城の関所 • 娘子関
La Passe de la Grande Muraille – Niangziguan

漢長城遺址
Ruins of the Great Wall of the Han Dynasty
漢代の長城跡
Vestiges de la Grande Muraille de la Dynastie des Han

俯視嘉峪關
A bird's-eye view of Jiayu Pass
嘉峪関を見おろす
Vue à vol d'oiseau de Jiayuguan

歷盡滄桑
The Great Wall has seen numerous battles
変遷をくりかえす長城
Une preuve de l'histoire

歴盡滄桑
The Great Wall has seen numerous battles
変遷をくりかえす長城
Une preuve de l'histoire

古城藝趣
Art of the Great Wall
古城の趣
L'art de la Grande Muraille

望京樓余輝
Wangjing Tower in afterglow
夕日の光が照らす望京楼
Wangjinglou sous des rayons du soleil couch-
ant

翻山越嶺
The Great Wall crosses many
山を登り峰を越す
La Grande Muraille le long des montagnes

▼ 慕田峪之夏
Mutianyu in summer
慕田峪の夏
Mutianyu en été

緑毯臥龍
Dragons on green blankets
緑に囲まれた長城
Dragons sur des couvertures vertes

金山嶺夕輝
Jinshanling under sun's glow
金山嶺の夕焼け
Jinshanling sous des rayons du soleil couchant

長城暮色
The Great Wall at sunset
長城の夕暮れ
La Grande Muraille au coucher du soleil

插箭嶺長城
The Great Wall at Chajianling
插箭嶺長城
La Grande Muraille à Chajianling

風起雲涌
The Great Wall at Jinshanling amidst clouds
長城の嵐
Nuages de la Grande Muraille

作者简介：

成大林　男　汉族　1942年出生　祖籍河北省大名县。1965年北京体育学院医疗保健专业本科毕业，毕业后到新华通讯社工作。现任新华通讯社新闻摄影编辑部主任记者。

　　他从事摄影工作近三十年，绝大部分精力倾注于对中国古代文化的摄影报导，特别从1978年以来，他全身心的从事长城的研究和摄影报道工作，他风餐露宿、翻山越岭，行程近十万华里，是目前我国文物考古和摄影界中见到长城最多的人。他为我国长城研究和宣传积累了宝贵而丰富的资料，不仅为报刊提供了大量的图片和文章，而且他个人或以他为主先后在国内、台湾、香港、美国出版了6本长城画册以及幻灯片、明信片、通俗读物等作品，国内几座大型长城博物馆展出的图片大部分都是他的作品。

　　他的工作从一开始就受到新闻界、摄影界和文物考古界的重视，得到了新华社及各地党政军部门的热情支持。最近，五羊自行车集团公司将协助他进行新的考察、摄影活动。各新闻单位对他进行了广泛的报道，1984年他被评为全国优秀新闻工作者，他现任中国长城学会常务理事、学术委员会副主任；受聘为中国嘉峪关长城研究会、山海关长城研究会、金山岭长城、嘉峪关长城博物馆、山海关长城博物馆、长城博物馆顾问；他还是中国摄影家协会、新闻摄影协会会员、远洋摄影协会艺术顾问。

〔京〕新登字146号

责任编辑：鲁　牧
主　　编：成大林
　　　　　舒　辉
摄　　影：成大林
装帧设计：石国强
翻　　译：余　波(英、法)
　　　　　赵家俊(日)

图书在版编目(CIP)数据

中国长城：汉、日、英、法对照／成大林，舒辉编；成大林摄.—北京：北京体育大学出版社，1994
ISBN 7-81003-893-1

Ⅰ.中…　Ⅱ.①成…　②舒…　③成…　Ⅲ.长成-中国-现代-摄影集-汉、日、英、法对照　Ⅳ.J426

中国版本图书馆CIP数据核字（94）第05486号

中国长城　　　　　　　　　　　成大林　舒辉编

北京体育大学出版社出版发行
(北京西郊圆明园东路)
新华书店总店北京发行所经销

开本：787×1092毫米　1/12印张：7　印数：5000
1994年5月第1版　　　1994年5月第1次印刷
ISBN 7—81003—893—1/J·189